HAL•LEONARD DRUM PLAY-ALONG

JIMI HENDRIX EXPERIENCE SMASH HITS

MW00782820

Tracking, mixing, and mastering by Jake Johnson
Drums by Scott Schroedl
Guitars by Doug Boduch
Bass by Tom McGirr
Keyboards by Warren Wiegratz

ISBN-13: 978-1-4234-1599-2
ISBN-10: 1-4234-1599-X

Visit Hal Leonard Online at www.halleonard.com

EXPERIENCE
HENDRIX
"A JIMI HENDRIX FAMILY COMPANY"

EXCLUSIVELY DISTRIBUTED BY

HAL•LEONARD®
CORPORATION

7777 W. BLUEMOUND RD. P.O. BOX 13819 MILWAUKEE, WI 53213

HAL•LEONARD

DRUM PLAY-ALONG™

VOL. II

JIMI HENDRIX EXPERIENCE
SMASH HITS

CONTENTS

Purple Haze

Words and Music by Jimi Hendrix

Intro
Moderate Rock ♩ = 106

Verse

1. Pur-ple haze ___ all in my brain. ___ Late-ly things, they don't

seem the same. Act-in' fun-ny, but I don't know why.

S'cuse me ____ while I kiss the sky.

Verse

2. Pur - ple haze ____ all a - round. ____ Don't know if I'm com - in'

up or down. Am I hap - py or in mis - er - y? What -

ev - er it is, __ that girl put a spell on me. ____

Help me! Help me! Oh, ____ no, ____ no!

Guitar Solo

5

Interlude

Verse

3. Pur - ple haze _____ all in my eyes, _____ uh,

don't know if it's ____ day or night. You got me blow - in',

blow-in' my mind. __ Is it to - mor - row or just the end of time?

Outro

Ooh. __ Help me.

Fire

Words and Music by Jimi Hendrix

Intro
Moderately fast Rock ♩ = 150

Verse

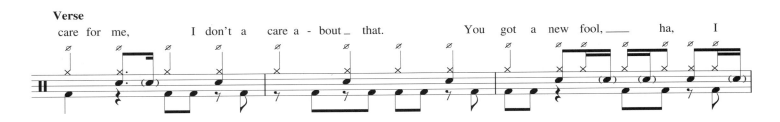

Chorus

Bridge

Guitar Solo

Interlude

That's what I'm talkin' a - bout. ___

Now, dig   this!   Ha!

Now lis- ten, ba - by!   3. You try to

Outro

Yeah! — You bet-ter move o - ver,

ba - by! I ain't gon - na hurt ya, ba - by!

Ah, — I ain't talk with your ol' la-dy. Ow!

Begin fade

Ah, — yes, this is Jim - i talk-in' to you!

Yeah, — ba-by!

Do, do, do, do, do, do!

Fade out

The Wind Cries Mary

Words and Music by Jimi Hendrix

Intro
Freely ♩ = 70

Verse
Moderately slow Rock ♩ = 78

1. Af - ter all the jacks _ are in their box - es, and the clowns have all _ gone to

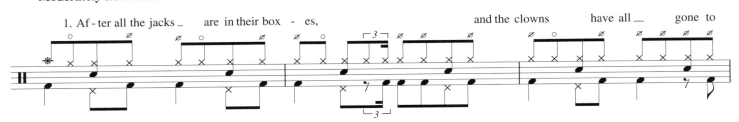

bed, _ you can hear hap-pi-ness stag-ger-in' _ on down the street, _

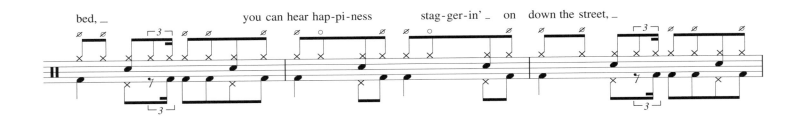

foot - prints dressed in red. _____ And the

wind _ whis - pers Mar - y.

Verse

Verse

3. The traf - fic lights, they turn, uh,   blue   to - mor - row, —   and

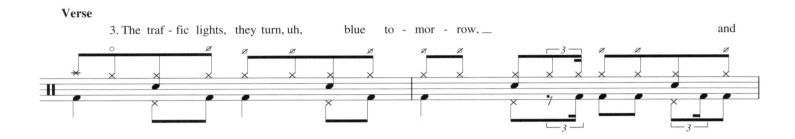

shine their emp - ti - ness   down —   on   my   bed. —   The   ti - ny

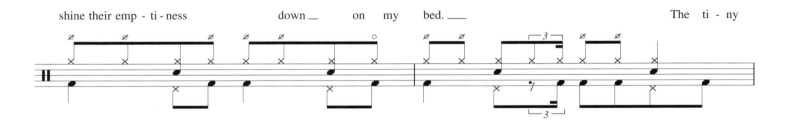

is   -   land —   sags   down -   stream ———   'cause   the

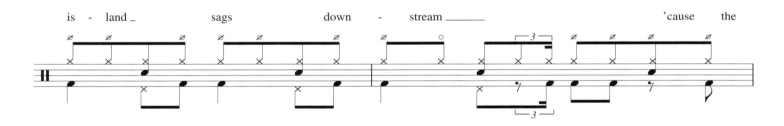

life   that   lived —   is,   is   dead. ———   And   the

wind —   screams   Mar - y.

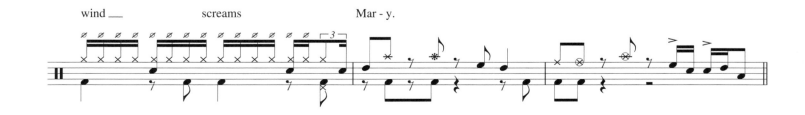

Verse

Can You See Me?

Words and Music by Jimi Hendrix

Intro
Moderate Rock ♩ = 132

1. Uh, can you see ___

Verse

___ me, ___ yeah,   beg-ging you ___ on my knee?

Whoa, yeah! ___   Can you see ___

___ me, ba - by,   beg-ging please ___ don't leave? ___

Al- right?   If you can

Guitar Solo

Ah,   yeah!

Verse

3. Ooh!   Uh, can   you hear   me   sing - in' this __ song   to

you?   Ah, __ you bet - ter o - pen up your __ ears, _____ ba - by!

Can   you   hear __ me, ba - by,   sing - in' this __ song   to

you?   Ah, _____ shucks!

20

Hey Joe

Words and Music by Billy Roberts

man.   Yeah!

I'm go - in' down to shoot my old la - dy   you know I caught her mess-in' 'round with an -

oth-er man. _   Huh!   And that ain't too   cool.

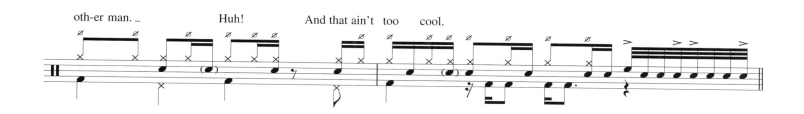

Verse

2. Uh, hey, ___ Joe, ___   I heard you ___ shot your

wom-an down, _ you shot her down, now. ___

Uh, hey, ___ Joe,   I heard you   shot   your old

la-dy down, _ you shot her down in the ground. _ Yeah! _

Yes, I _ did, I shot her, you know I caught her mess-in''round,

mess-in' 'round town. _

R L R R L R L R L L R L R R L R L L L R L R R L R L L R L R R L R L L

Um, yes, I did, I shot her, you know I caught my old la - dy mess-in' 'round

town. _ And I gave her the gun, I shot her! _

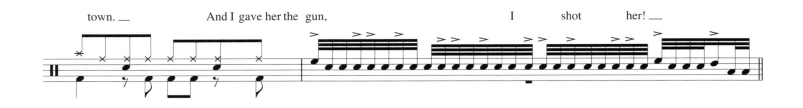

Guitar Solo

Al - right! _   Shoot her one more time a - gain, _ ba - by!

Yeah!   Ah,   dig it!

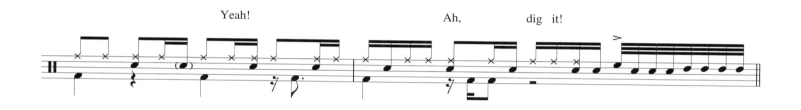

Interlude

Ah!   Ah!

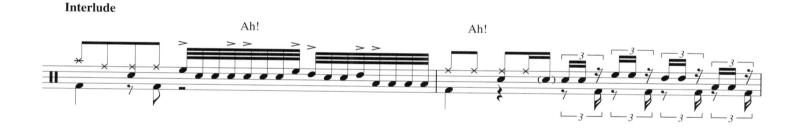

Ooh, al - right! _

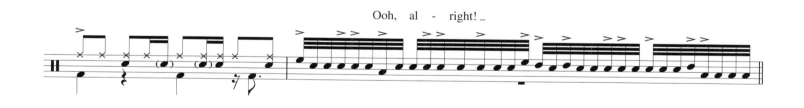

Verse

3. Hey, _____ Joe,   said now,   uh, where you   gon - na run

to now,____ where you gon-na run   to?____   Yeah.

Hey,_____   Joe,____   I said,   where you gon-na   run__

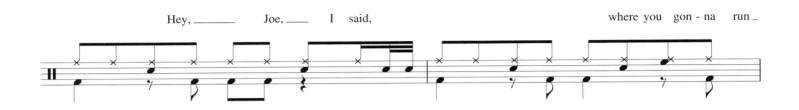

__ to   now,__ where you,   where you gon-na go?   Well, dig it!

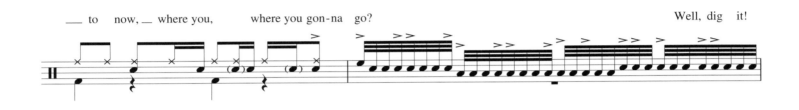

I'm go-in' way down   south, __   way   down_____   to

Mex-i-co__ way! __   Al - right! __

I'm go-in' way down   south, __   way down ___ where   I_____

can be free! Ain't no one ___ gon-na find me, babe!

Ain't no hang - man gon - na,   he ain't gon-na put a rope a - round

me! You bet-ter be - lieve ___ it right ___ now! ___ I got - ta go ___ now!

Begin fade

Hey, __ hey, hey, __ Joe,   you bet - ter run ___ on ___ down!

Good - bye, ev -'ry - bod - y.   Ow!

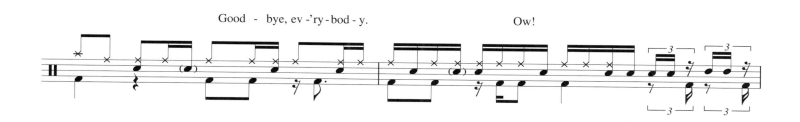

Fade out

Hey, _ hey, _ Joe, _ what'd I say,   run on ___ down!

All Along the Watchtower

Words and Music by Bob Dylan

Intro
Moderately ♩ = 112

Verse

1. There must be some kind a way out-ta here, _____ say the jok-er to the thief. ___

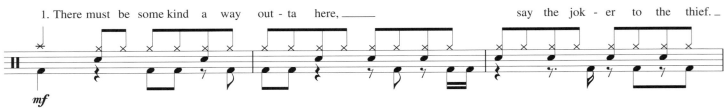

_____ There's too much con-fu-sion, _____ na.

I can't get no re-lief. _____ Busi-ness men, they, ah, ah,

who feel that life _ is but a joke. _____ But, uh, but you and I, we've been _

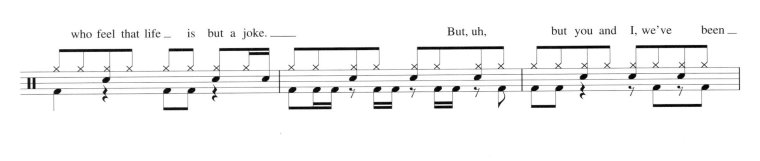

_ through that, but, ah, and this is not our fate. _____

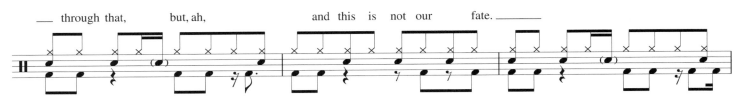

So let us not talk false - ly now, the ho - ur's get - tin' _ late, _

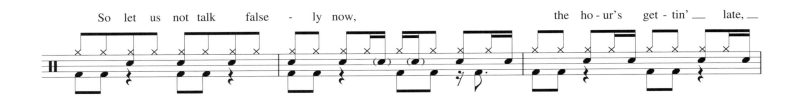

_ ah. Hey! _____

Guitar Solo

ff

Interlude

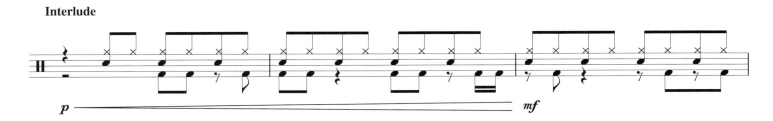

p _____ mf

30

Hey!

Guitar Solo

Verse

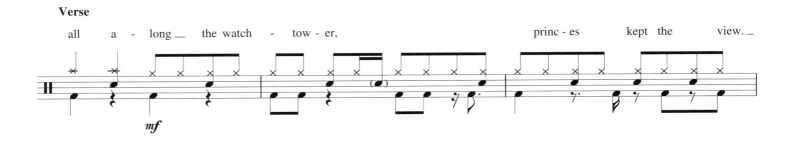

Outro

All a - long   the watch - tow -

er   they ____ say   come

in.   Have you ev - er?   Don't be way out

here.   Yeah. ____

____   Ah,

babe.   Well,

Fade out

all   a - long ___ the watch - tow - er. ___

Stone Free

Words and Music by Jimi Hendrix

Intro
Moderate Rock ♩ = 132

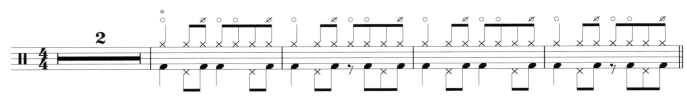

*w/ overdubbed quarter notes on cowbell till Pre-Chorus.

Verse

1. Ev - 'ry day in the week I'm ___ in a dif - f'rent cit - y.

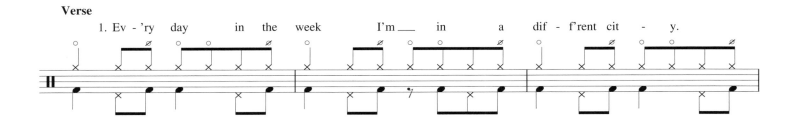

Ooh, if I stay ___ too long ___ the peo - ple try to

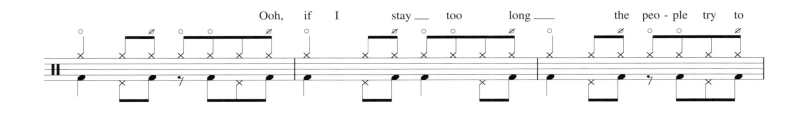

pull ___ me down. They talk a - bout me like a dog,

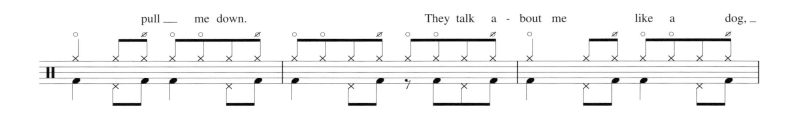

___ talk a - bout the clothes ___ I ___ wear. But

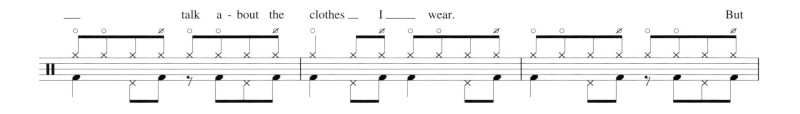

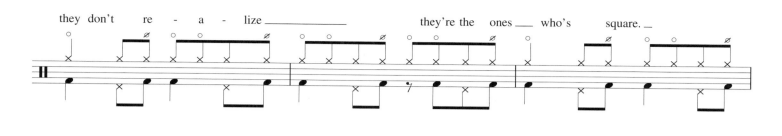

they don't re - a - lize _____ they're the ones ___ who's square. __

Pre-Chorus

Hey! That's why _____ you ___ can't _ hold _

__ me down. I ___ don't wan - na be ___ down! _____

I got to move on! _ Ow! ___ Ah!

Chorus

Stone free, to do what I ___ please. _ Stone free, to

ride _____ the breeze. Stone free! I can't stay! ___ I

got - ta, got - ta, got - ta get a - way ___ right now. Yeah! _

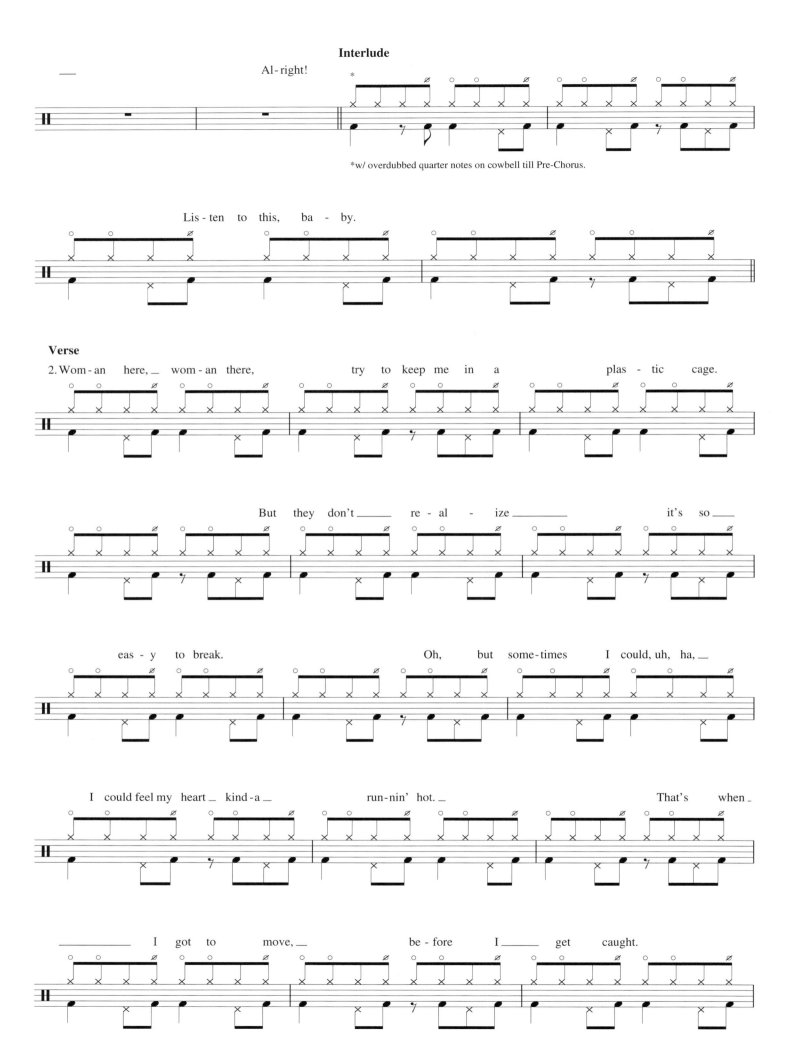

Interlude

*w/ overdubbed quarter notes on cowbell till Pre-Chorus.

36

Pre-Chorus

Guitar Solo

Yeah!

Uh, huh!

Chorus

Yeah! _____ I _____ said, ___ stone free, to ride _____ the breeze.

Stone free, to do what I _____ please! Stone free! Uh,

Crosstown Traffic

Words and Music by Jimi Hendrix

Intro
Moderately ♩ = 116

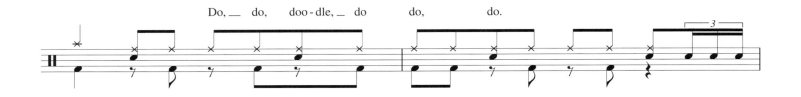

Do, ___ do, doo - dle, ___ do do, do.

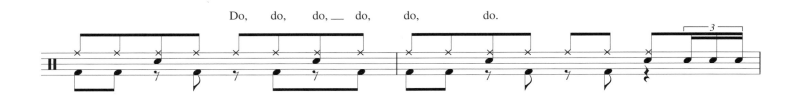

Do, do, do, ___ do, do, do.

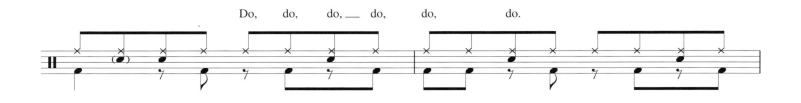

Do, do, do, ___ do, do, do.

Do, do, do, do, do, do, ___ do, do, do, do.

Verse

Verse

Chorus

Guitar Solo

Chorus

44

Manic Depression

Words and Music by Jimi Hendrix

Intro
Moderate Rock ♩ = 148

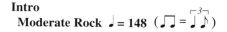

Verse

1. Man - ic de - pres - sion __ is

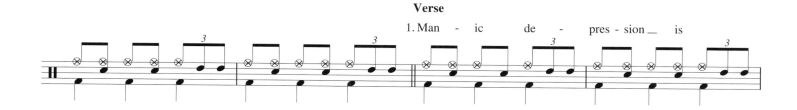

touch - in' my soul. _____

I ___ know what I ___ want __ but I, I just don't ___

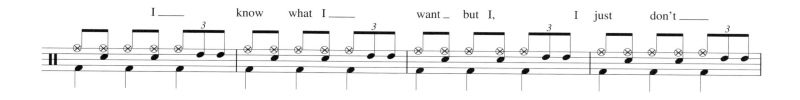

know ___ how to, heh, go a - bout get - tin' it.

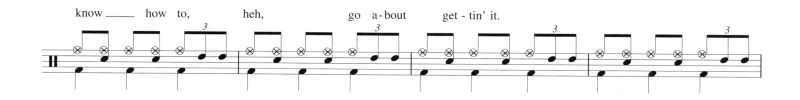

Feel - in', sweet feel - in' drops from my fin - gers,

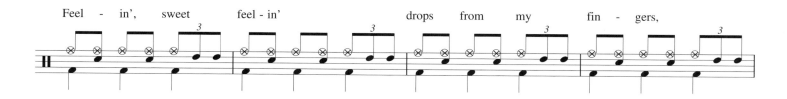

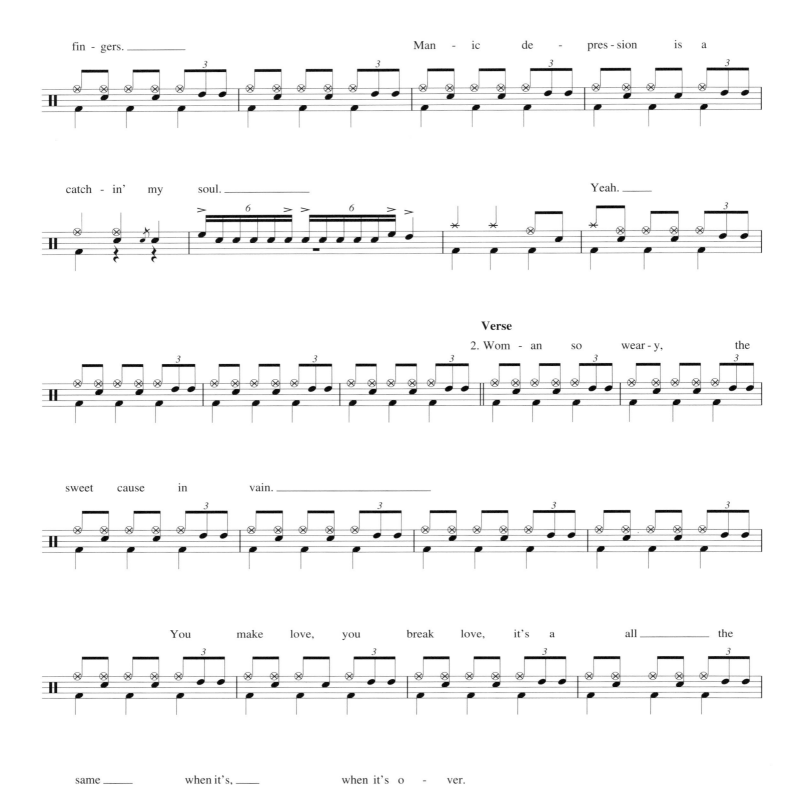

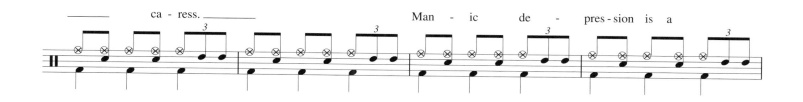

ca - ress. _____ Man - ic de - pres - sion is a

frus - trat - ing mess. Oo, ow! _____

Interlude
Do, _____ do,

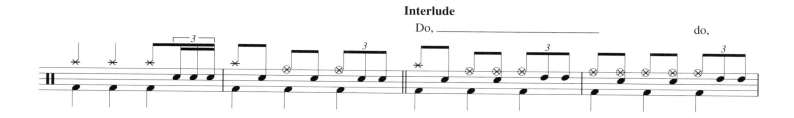

do, _____ do, _____ do, do.

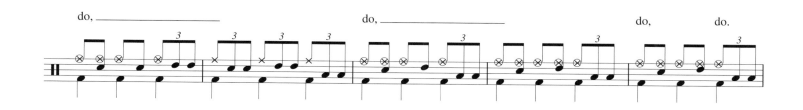

Guitar Solo

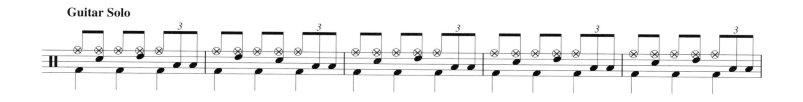

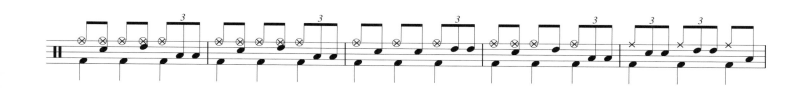

Cry ___ on ___ gui-tar.

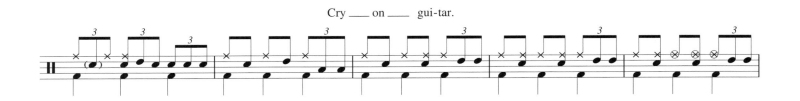

3. Well, I ___

Verse

think I'll go turn my-self off ___ and, uh, uh, huh, go on ___ down. ___

Huh! All the way down. Real - ly ain't no

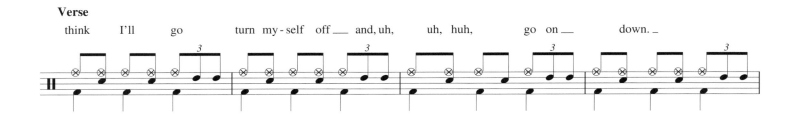

use ___ in me ___ hang - in' a - round ___ in, uh, huh, your ___

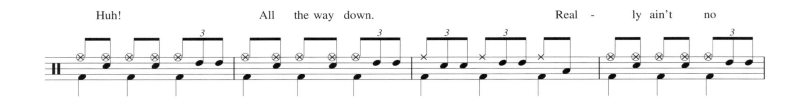

kind of scene. _____ Mu - sic, sweet mu - sic, I

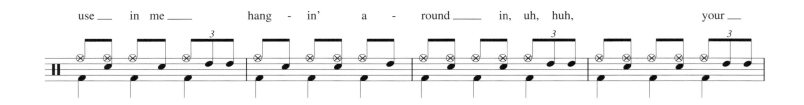

*Played as even eighth notes.

**Accidentally hit sticks.

Mu - sic, sweet

mu - sic, sweet   mu - sic.   Yeah! _

Do, _____   oo, _____

oo.

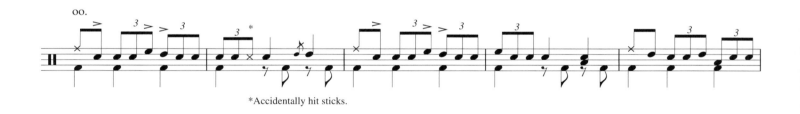

*Accidentally hit sticks.

Free time

Hmm, hmm, hmm.

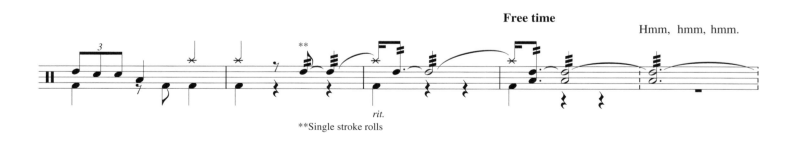

rit.
**Single stroke rolls

De - press...

Remember

Words and Music by Jimi Hendrix

Intro
Moderately slow Rock ♩ = 98

- ber.   Yeah! ___   Got   to   re - mem -

ber, Lord. _   Come on ___ back in, uh,   come on ___ back in ___ my arms. _____

Make ev - 'ry-thing ___ back to - geth-er.

Outro

Ba   -   by,   hur - ry up, now.

Can you   hear ___ me call - ing you ___   back   a - gain, _   now? _____

Begin fade

C' - mon,   ba - by!   Stop   jiv - in' a - round!

Fade out

Hur - ry home, _____ hur - ry home, _   uh.

Red House

Words and Music by Jimi Hendrix

Lord, there's a red house __ o - ver yon-der. __ Lord, that's where __ my ba by stays. __

Ain't __ been home to see my __ ba - by in 'bout nine-ty-nine and one half days. __

2. Wait a

Verse

min - ute, some-thing's wrong here, __ the key won't un-lock this door. __

Wait a min-ute, some-thing's wrong. __ Lord, have mer-cy, this key won't un-lock this

door.   Some-thing's go-in' wrong here.   I have a bad, __

__ bad __ feel - in',   uh, _____   that my ba - by   don't live here no

more.   That's al - right, I still got my gui-tar. Look out, now! _

Guitar Solo

Yeah! __

That's al - right! _

3. Well, I might as well, uh, __

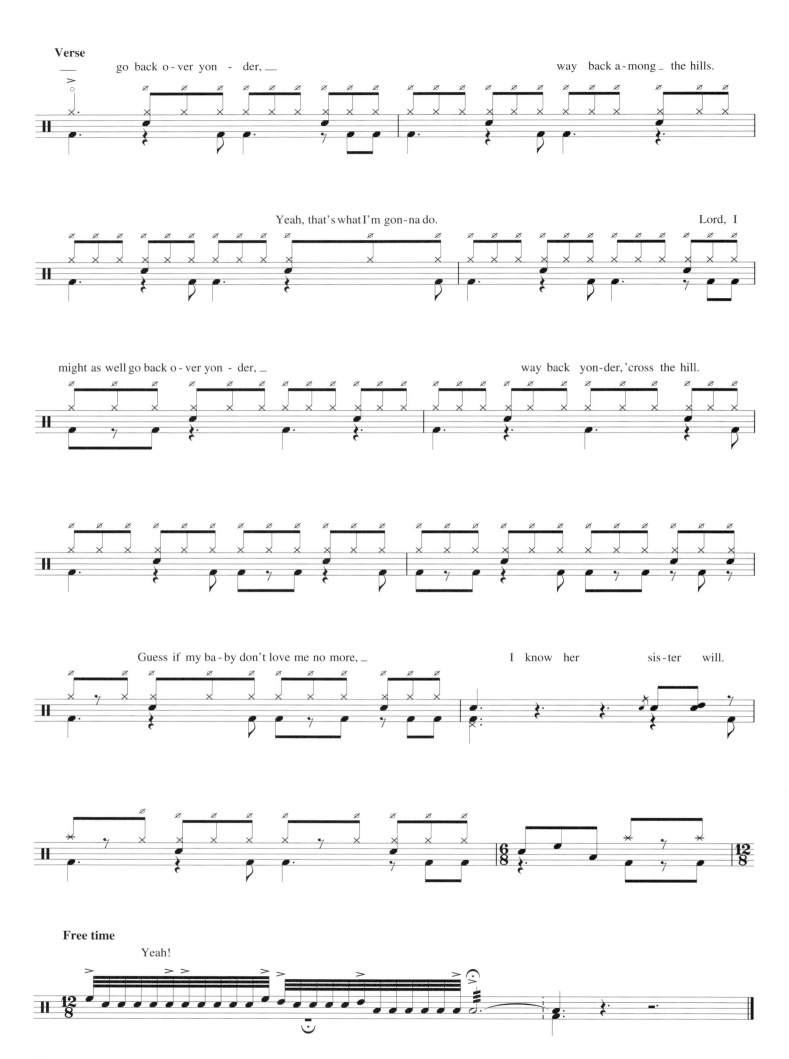

Foxey Lady

Words and Music by Jimi Hendrix

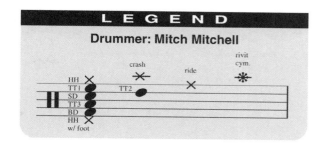

Intro
Moderate Rock ♩ = 96

Fox - y!   Fox - y!

Verse

1. Uh, you know ___ you a ___   cute lit - tle ___ heart - break - er, ___ ha!   Fox - y!

Yeah!   And you know ___ you a ___   sweet lit - tle ___ love ___ mak - er,

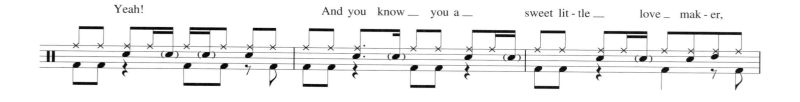

Chorus

huh!   Fox - y!   I wan - na take you home, ___

___ uh, huh!   Yeah! ___   I won't   do you no harm, ___ no. ___ Ha!

mine,　　all mine. ___　　　　　　　　　　　　　　　Fox - y ___ la - dy! ___　　　　　　　　　　　　Here I　　come! ___

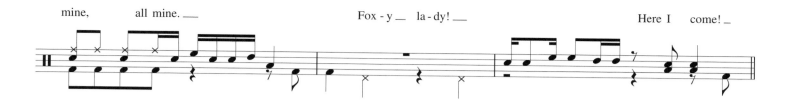

Guitar Solo

Fox - y　　　　la - dy!

Fox - y　　　la - dy!　　　　　　　　　　　　　　　　　　　　　　　　　Fox - y.　　　Fox - y!

Fox - y!　　　　　　　　Yeah!

Chorus

I'm　　gon - na take you home, ___　　uh, huh!

I won't do you no harm, ___　　　　　　　　　　　　no. ___

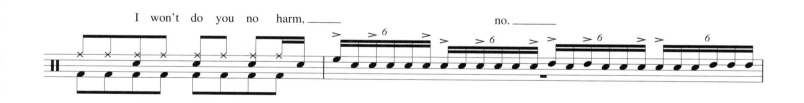

You got - ta be all　　mine,　　all ___ mine. ___　　　　　　Fox - y la - dy! ___

61

Free time　　　　　　　　　　　　　　　　　　　　　　　　　　**A tempo**

Outro

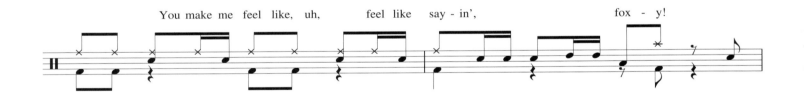

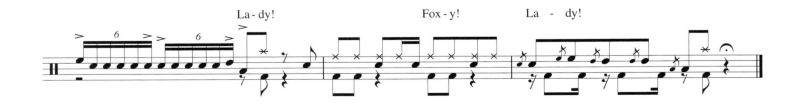

HAL•LEONARD DRUM PLAY•ALONG™

Play your favorite songs quickly and easily with the *Drum Play-Along™* series. Just follow the drum notation, listen to the CD to hear how the drums should sound, then play along using the separate backing tracks. The lyrics are also included for quick reference. The audio CD is playable on any CD player. For PC and Mac computer users, the CD is enhanced so you can adjust the recording to any tempo without changing the pitch!

Book/CD Packs

VOLUME 1 – POP/ROCK
Hurts So Good • Message in a Bottle • No Reply at All • Owner of a Lonely Heart • Peg • Rosanna • Separate Ways (Worlds Apart) • Swingtown.
00699742   Book/CD Pack $12.95

VOLUME 2 – CLASSIC ROCK
Barracuda • Come Together • Mississippi Queen • Radar Love • Space Truckin' • Walk This Way • White Room • Won't Get Fooled Again.
00699741   Book/CD Pack $12.95

VOLUME 3 – HARD ROCK
Bark at the Moon • Detroit Rock City • Living After Midnight • Panama • Rock You like a Hurricane • Run to the Hills • Smoke on the Water • War Pigs (Interpolating Luke's Wall).
00699743   Book/CD Pack $12.95

VOLUME 4 – MODERN ROCK
Chop Suey! • Duality • Here to Stay • Judith • Nice to Know You • Nookie • One Step Closer • Whatever.
00699744   Book/CD Pack $12.95

VOLUME 5 – FUNK
Cissy Strut • Cold Sweat, Part 1 • Fight the Power, Part 1 • Flashlight • Pick Up the Pieces • Shining Star • Soul Vaccination • Superstition.
00699745   Book/CD Pack $12.95

Prices, contents and availability subject to change without notice and may vary outside the US.

FOR MORE INFORMATION, SEE YOUR LOCAL MUSIC DEALER,
OR WRITE TO:

HAL•LEONARD®
CORPORATION
7777 W. BLUEMOUND RD. P.O. BOX 13819 MILWAUKEE, WI 53213
Visit Hal Leonard Online at
www.halleonard.com